Treasure Hunter

By Susan Koehler
Cover Illustrated By Ken Hooper
Color By Lance Borde
Interior Illustrated By Shepherd Hendrix

ROURKE PUBLISHING
Vero Beach, Florida 32964

www.rourkepublishing.com

Edited by Katherine M. Thal and Meg Greve
Cover Illustrated By Ken Hooper
Color Color By Lance Bord
Interior Illustrated by Shepherd Hendrix
Art Direction and Page Layout by Renee Brady

Photo Credits: ©Dirk-Jan Mattaav: title page, pgs. 26-32 (background); © Aleksandrs Marinicevs: p. 26; © DurdenImages: p. 27; © Kevin Panizza: p. 28 (top); © Deborah Cheramie: p. 28 (bottom)

Library of Congress Cataloging-in-Publication Data

Koehler, Susan, 1963-
  Treasure hunter / Susan Koehler.
     p. cm. -- (Jobs that rock graphic illustrated)
  Includes bibliographical references and index.
  ISBN 978-1-60694-374-8 (alk. paper)
  ISBN 978-1-60694-557-5 (soft cover)
 1. Treasure troves--Comic books, strips, etc. 2. Treasure troves--Vocational guidance--Juvenile literature. Title
  G525+
                        2009020484

Printed in the USA
CG/CG

www.rourkepublishing.com - rourke@rourkepublishing.com
Post Office Box 643328 Vero Beach, Florida 32964

Table of Contents

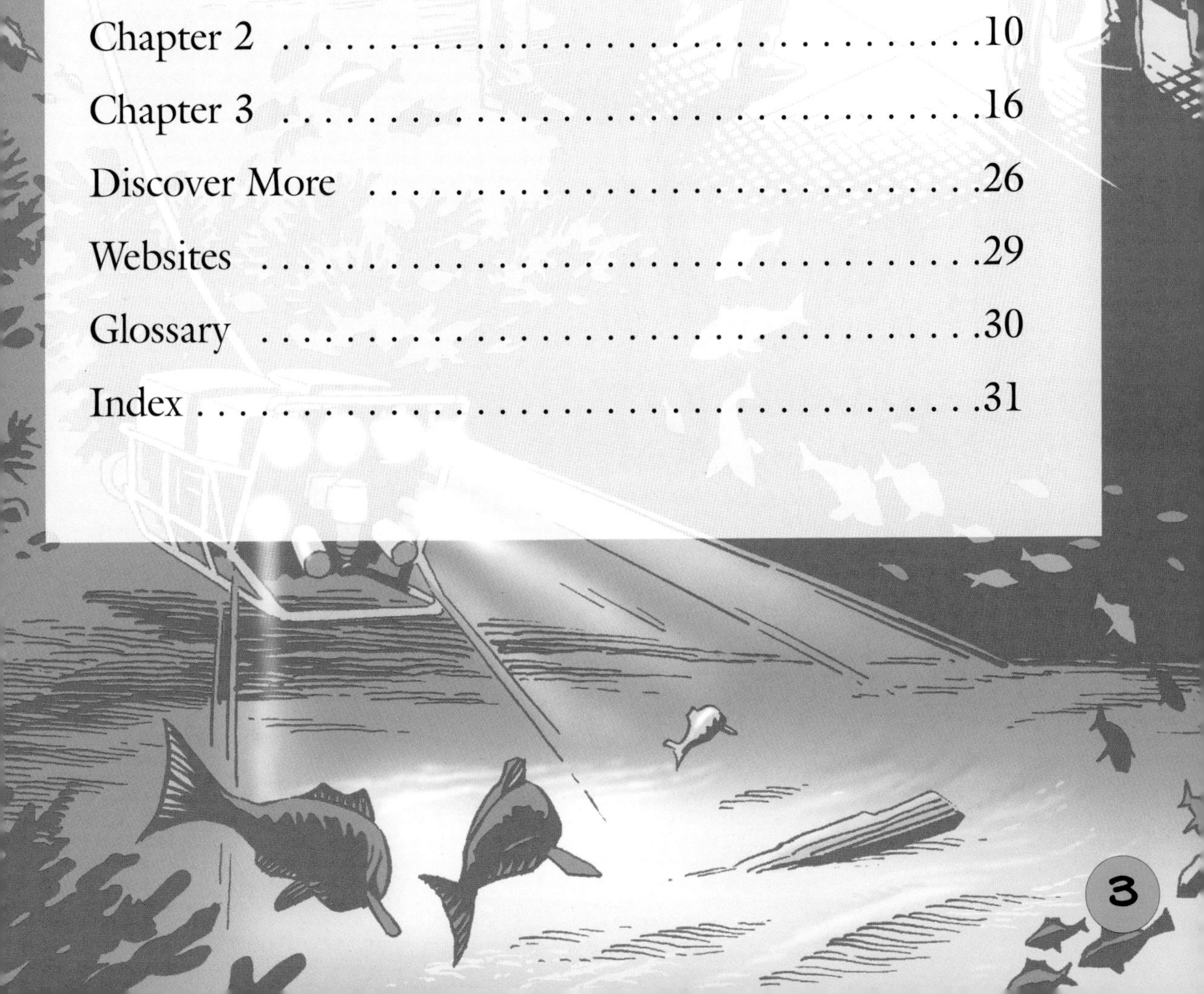

Tyler

Tyler is a ten-year-old boy who wants to experience the exciting world of treasure hunting.

Fran West

Fran West is Tyler and Shelby's mom.

Dylan Lamont

Dylan Lamont is a real treasure hunter and Fran's friend.

Shelby

Shelby is Tyler's twelve-year-old sister who soon finds treasure hunting exciting, too.

CHAPTER 1

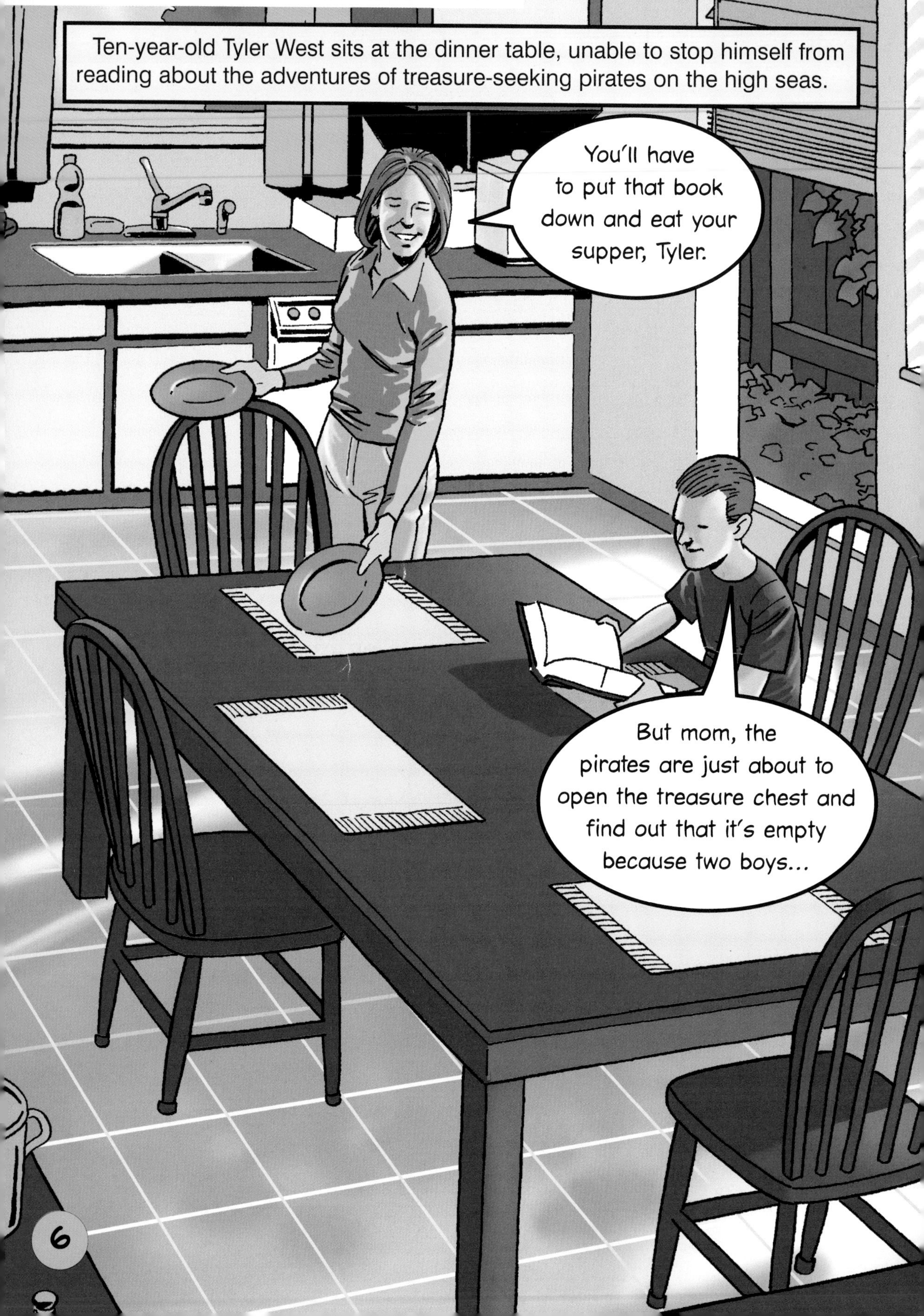
Ten-year-old Tyler West sits at the dinner table, unable to stop himself from reading about the adventures of treasure-seeking pirates on the high seas.
You'll have to put that book down and eat your supper, Tyler.
But mom, the pirates are just about to open the treasure chest and find out that it's empty because two boys...

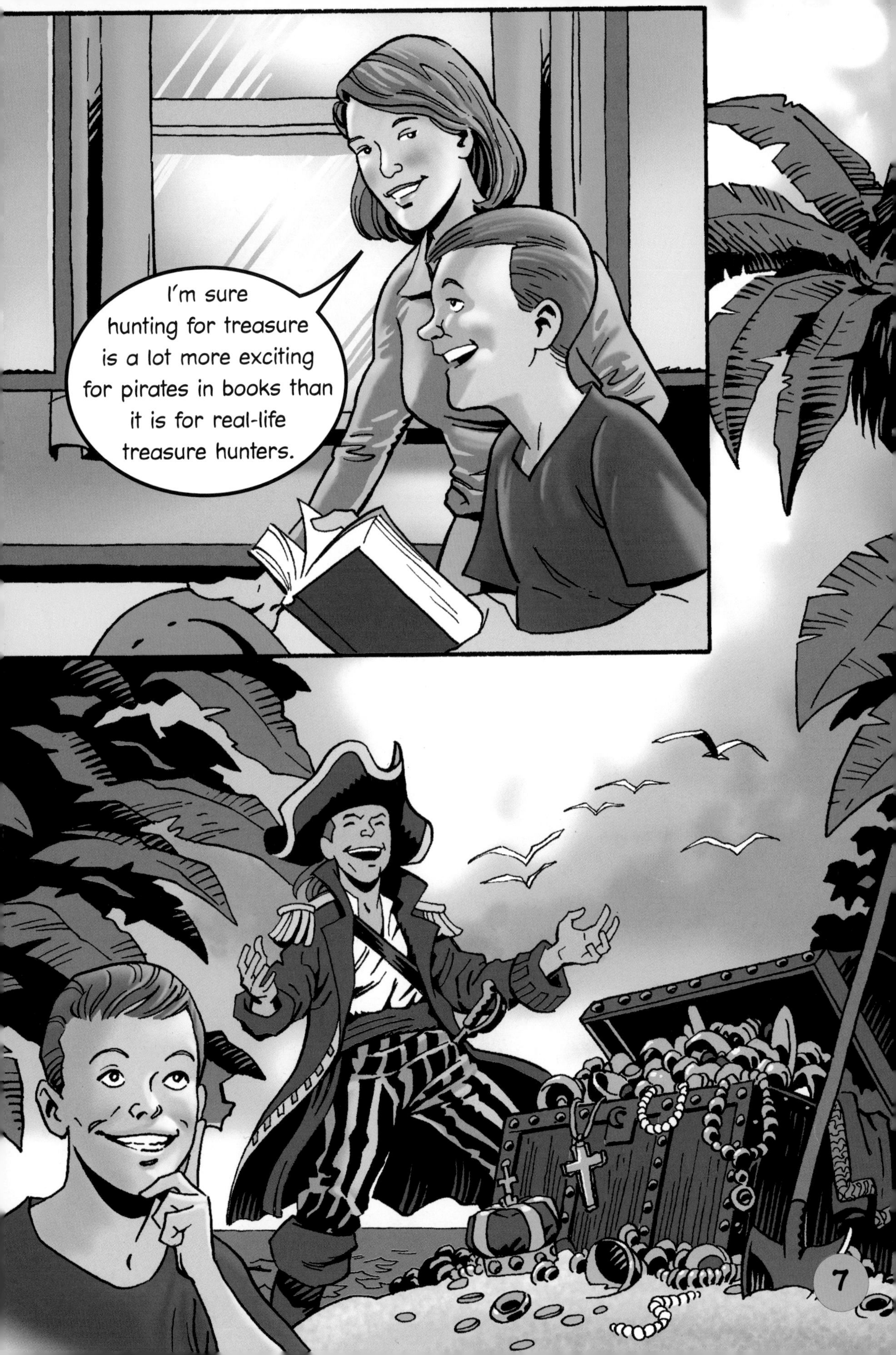
I'm sure hunting for treasure is a lot more exciting for pirates in books than it is for real-life treasure hunters.

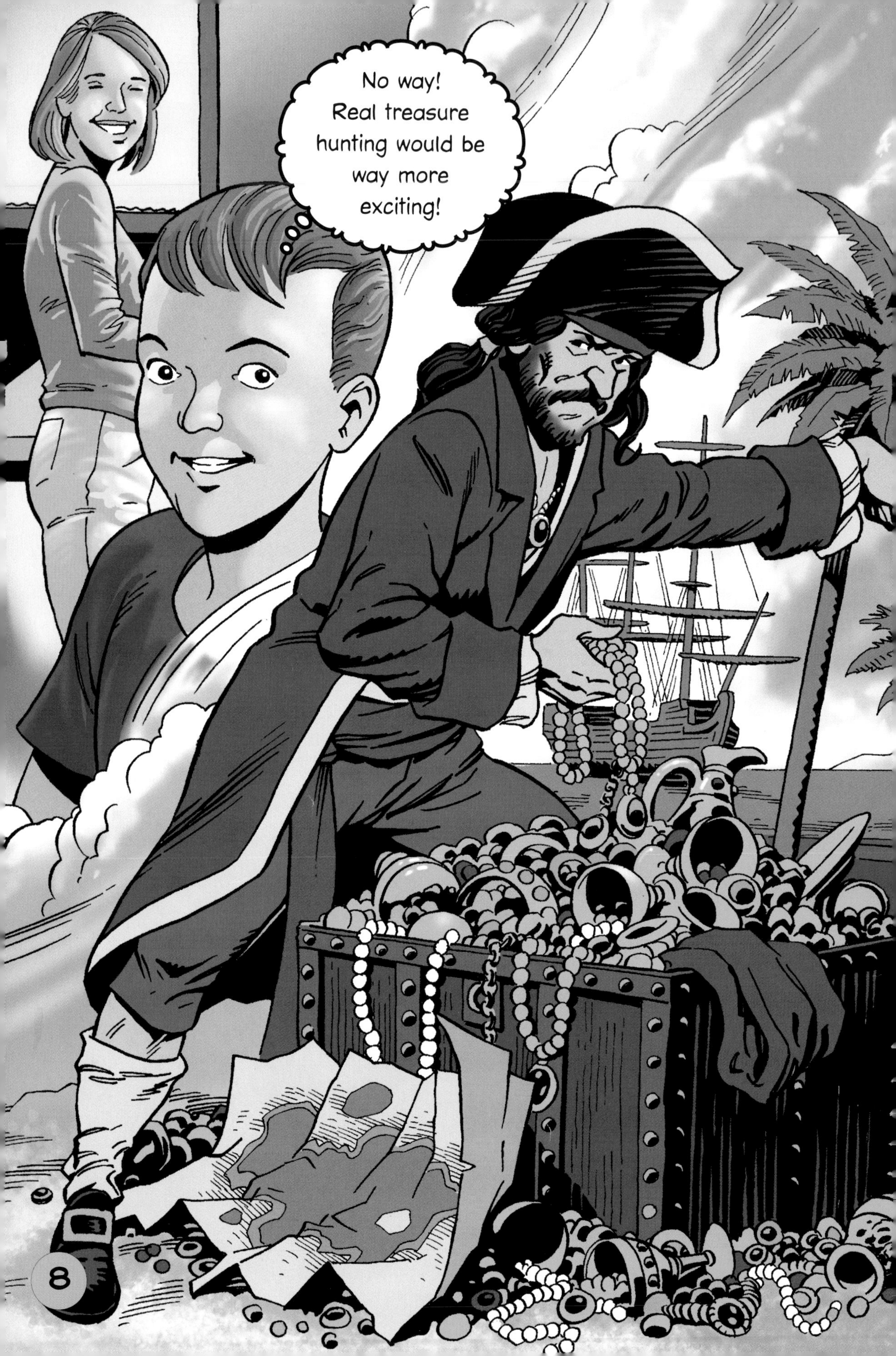
No way! Real treasure hunting would be way more exciting!

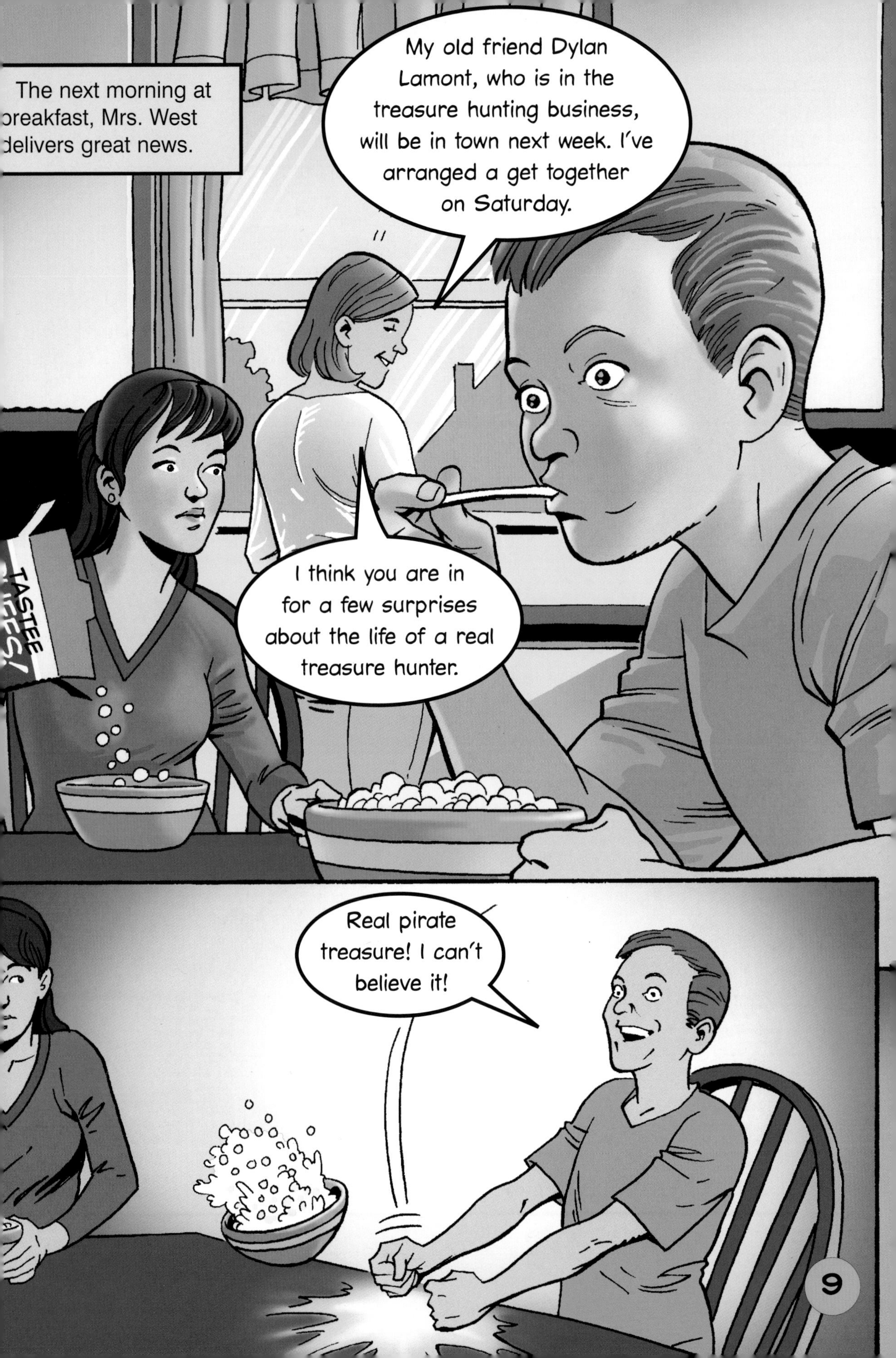
The next morning at breakfast, Mrs. West delivers great news.
My old friend Dylan Lamont, who is in the treasure hunting business, will be in town next week. I've arranged a get together on Saturday.
I think you are in for a few surprises about the life of a real treasure hunter.
Real pirate treasure! I can't believe it!

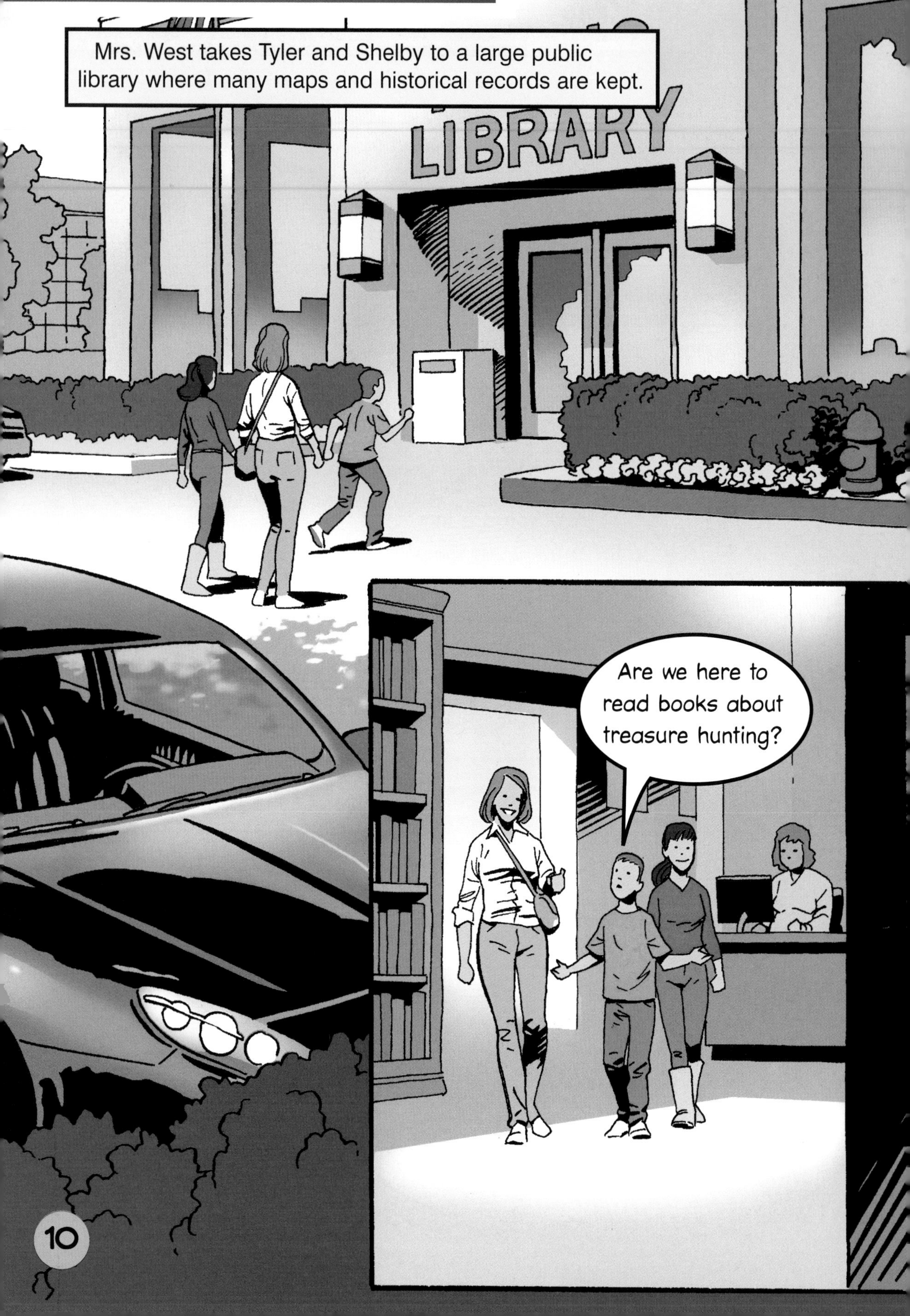
Mrs. West takes Tyler and Shelby to a large public library where many maps and historical records are kept.
LIBRARY
Are we here to read books about treasure hunting?

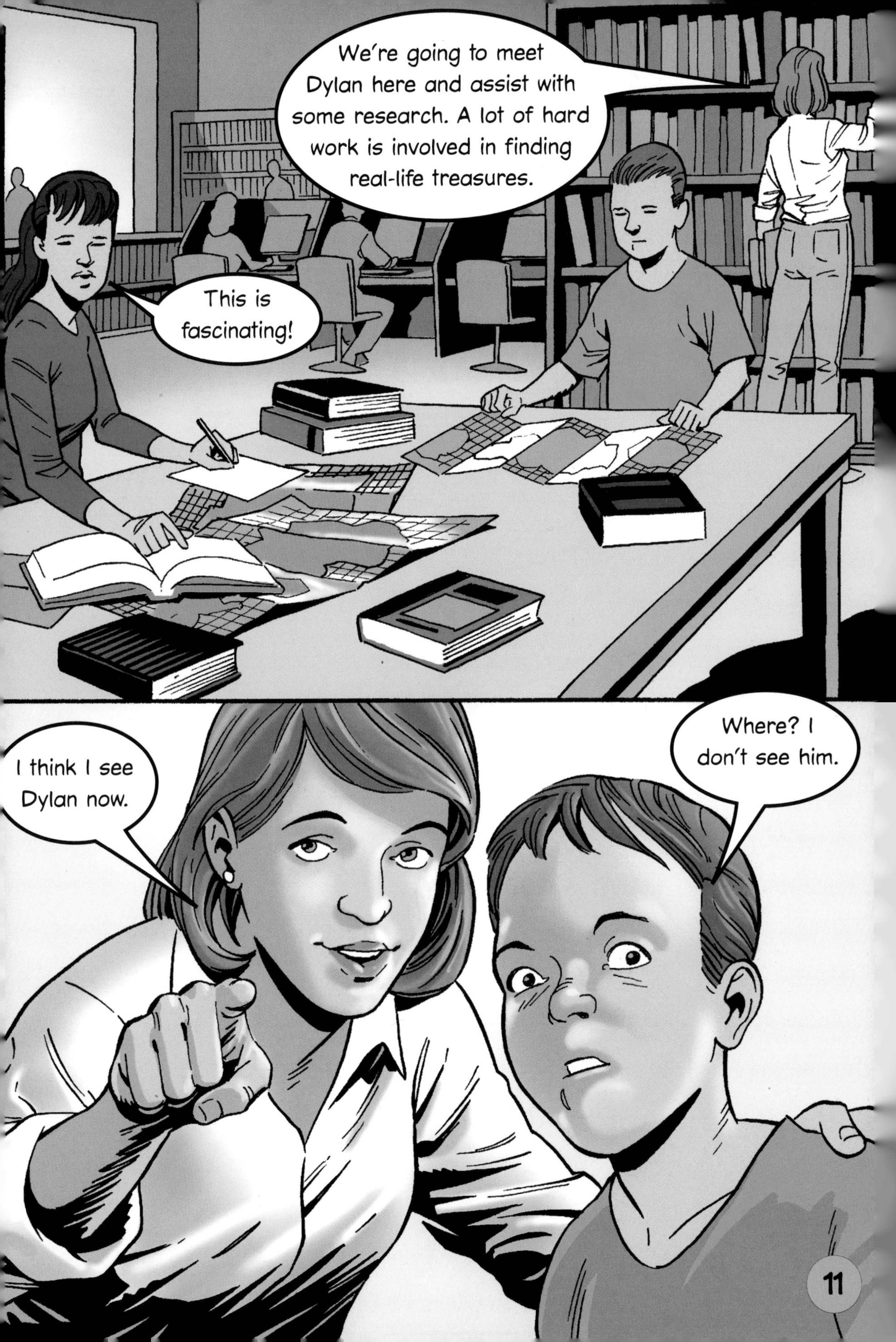
We're going to meet Dylan here and assist with some research. A lot of hard work is involved in finding real-life treasures.
This is fascinating!
I think I see Dylan now.
Where? I don't see him.

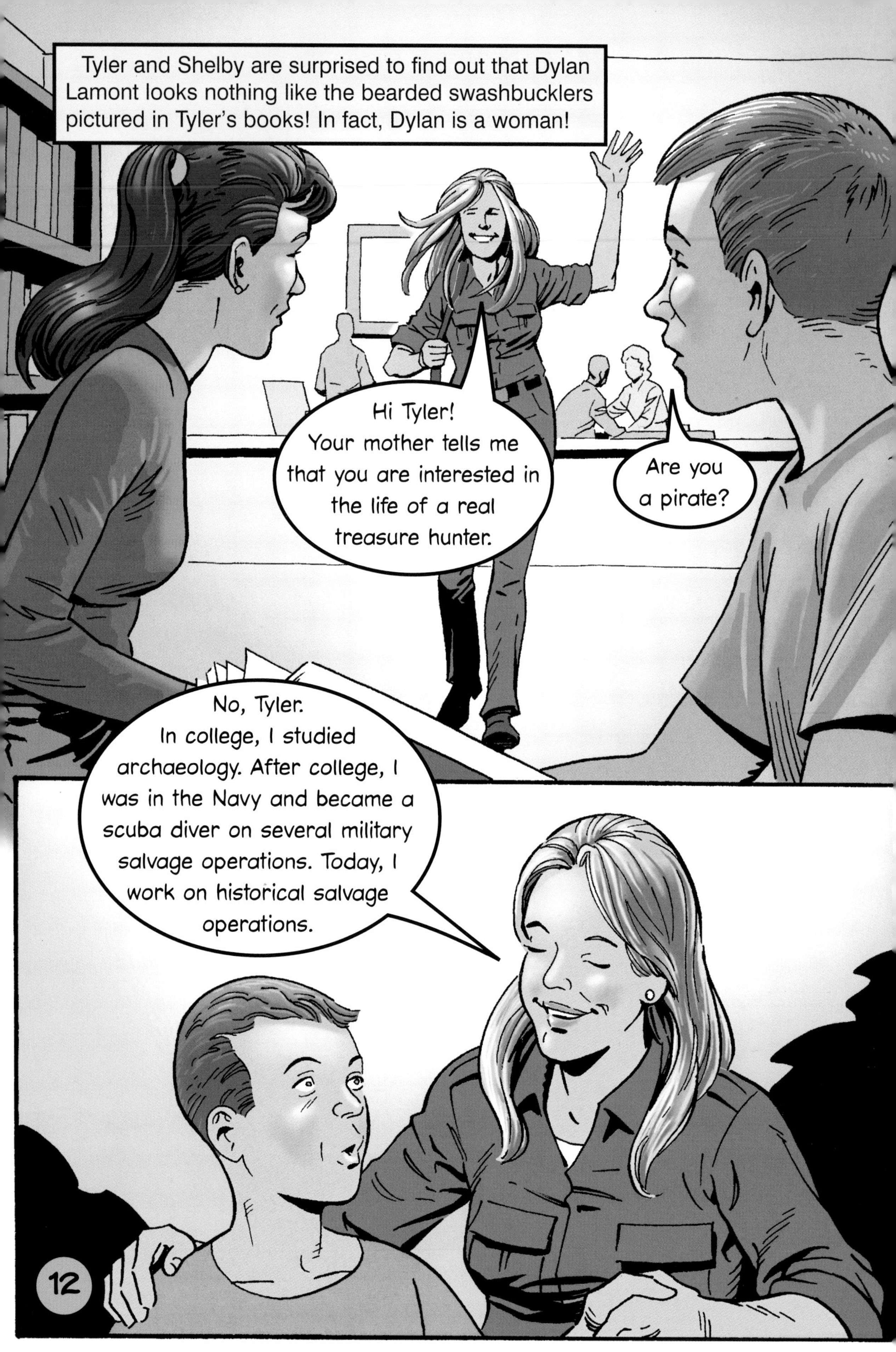
Tyler and Shelby are surprised to find out that Dylan Lamont looks nothing like the bearded swashbucklers pictured in Tyler's books! In fact, Dylan is a woman!
Hi Tyler! Your mother tells me that you are interested in the life of a real treasure hunter.
Are you a pirate?
No, Tyler. In college, I studied archaeology. After college, I was in the Navy and became a scuba diver on several military salvage operations. Today, I work on historical salvage operations.

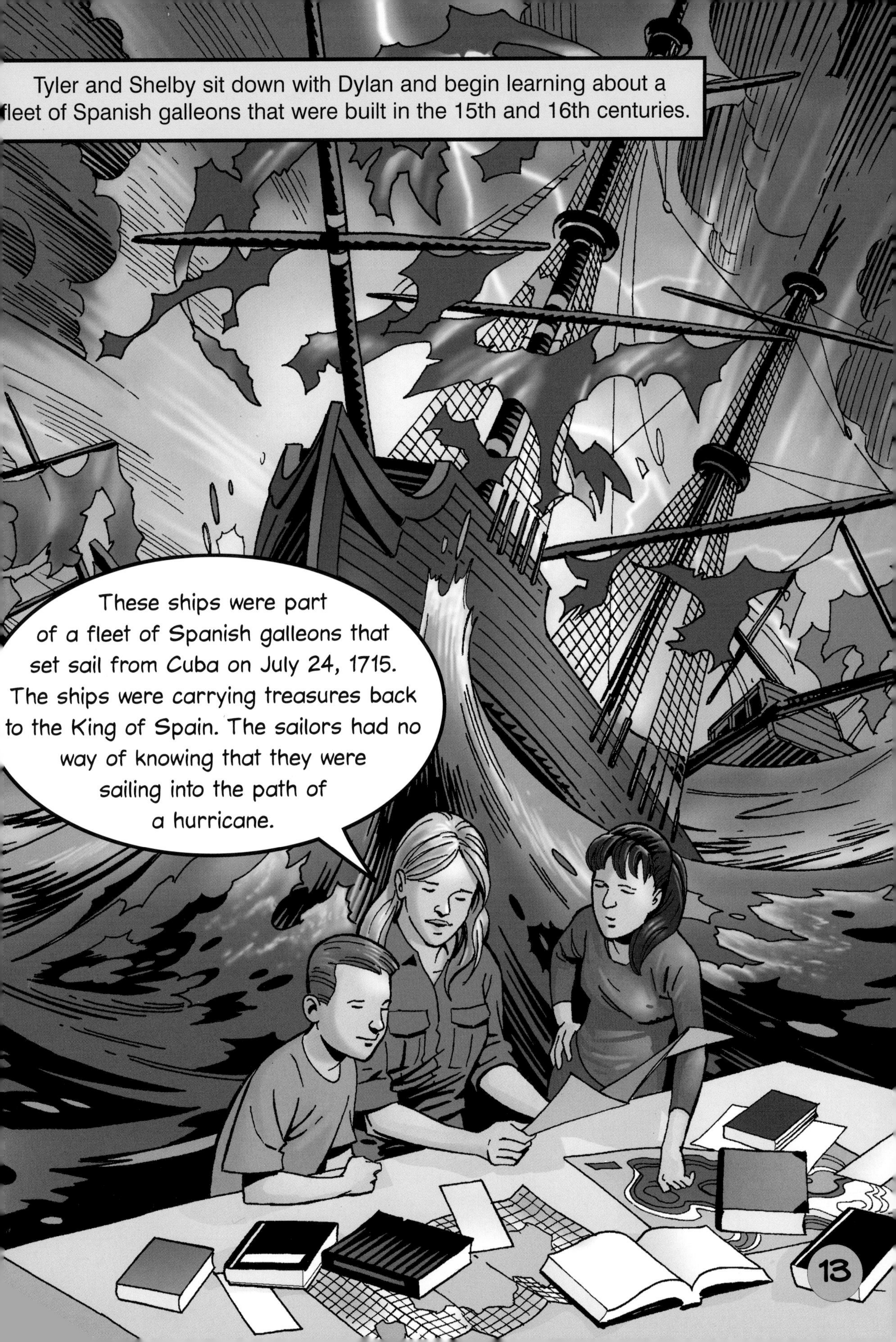
Tyler and Shelby sit down with Dylan and begin learning about a fleet of Spanish galleons that were built in the 15th and 16th centuries.
These ships were part of a fleet of Spanish galleons that set sail from Cuba on July 24, 1715. The ships were carrying treasures back to the King of Spain. The sailors had no way of knowing that they were sailing into the path of a hurricane.

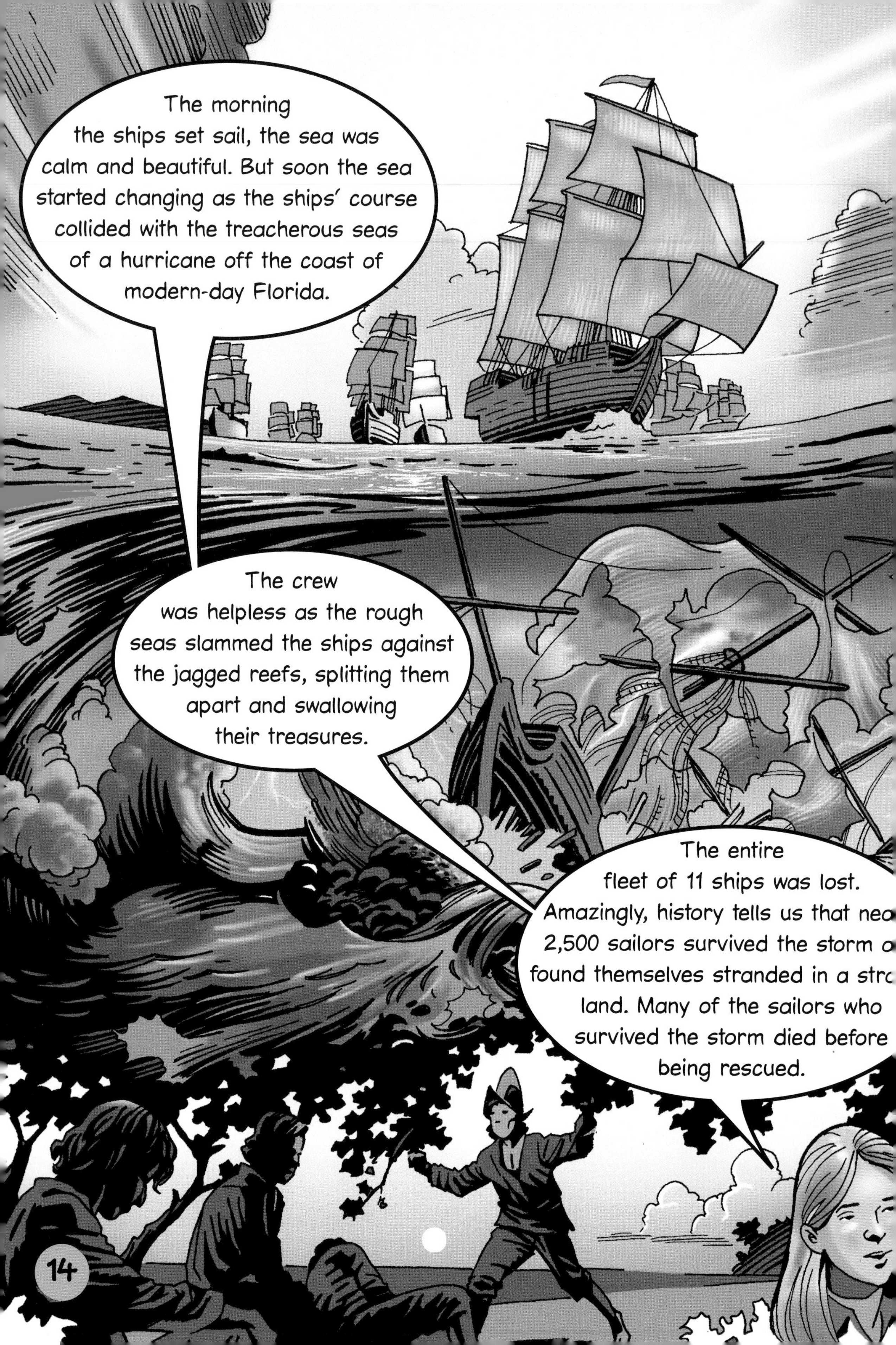
The morning the ships set sail, the sea was calm and beautiful. But soon the sea started changing as the ships' course collided with the treacherous seas of a hurricane off the coast of modern-day Florida.
The crew was helpless as the rough seas slammed the ships against the jagged reefs, splitting them apart and swallowing their treasures.
The entire fleet of 11 ships was lost. Amazingly, history tells us that nea 2,500 sailors survived the storm a found themselves stranded in a stra land. Many of the sailors who survived the storm died before being rescued.

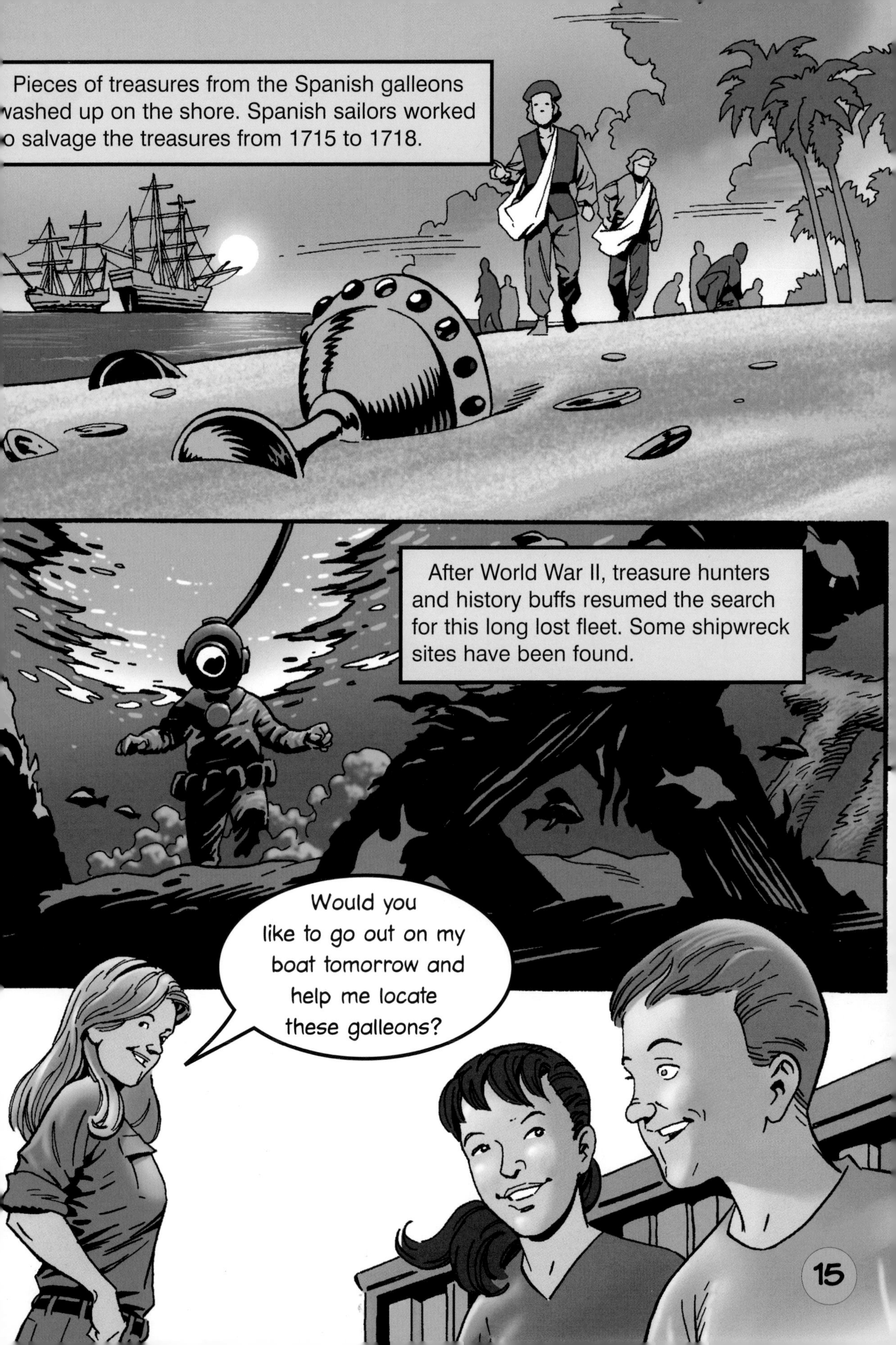
Pieces of treasures from the Spanish galleons vashed up on the shore. Spanish sailors worked o salvage the treasures from 1715 to 1718.
After World War II, treasure hunters and history buffs resumed the search for this long lost fleet. Some shipwreck sites have been found.
Would you like to go out on my boat tomorrow and help me locate these galleons?

CHAPTER 3

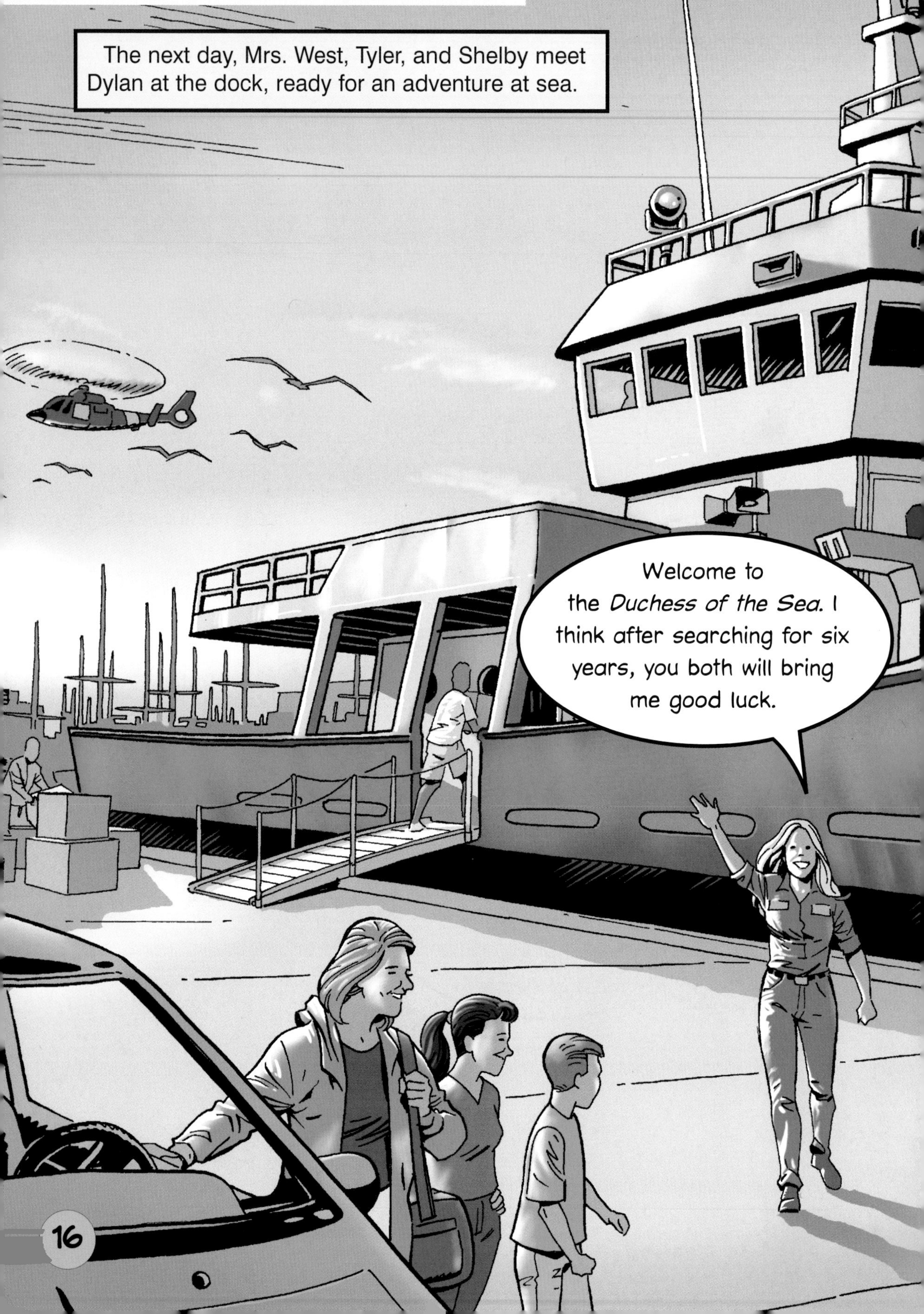
The next day, Mrs. West, Tyler, and Shelby meet Dylan at the dock, ready for an adventure at sea.
Welcome to the *Duchess of the Sea.* I think after searching for six years, you both will bring me good luck.

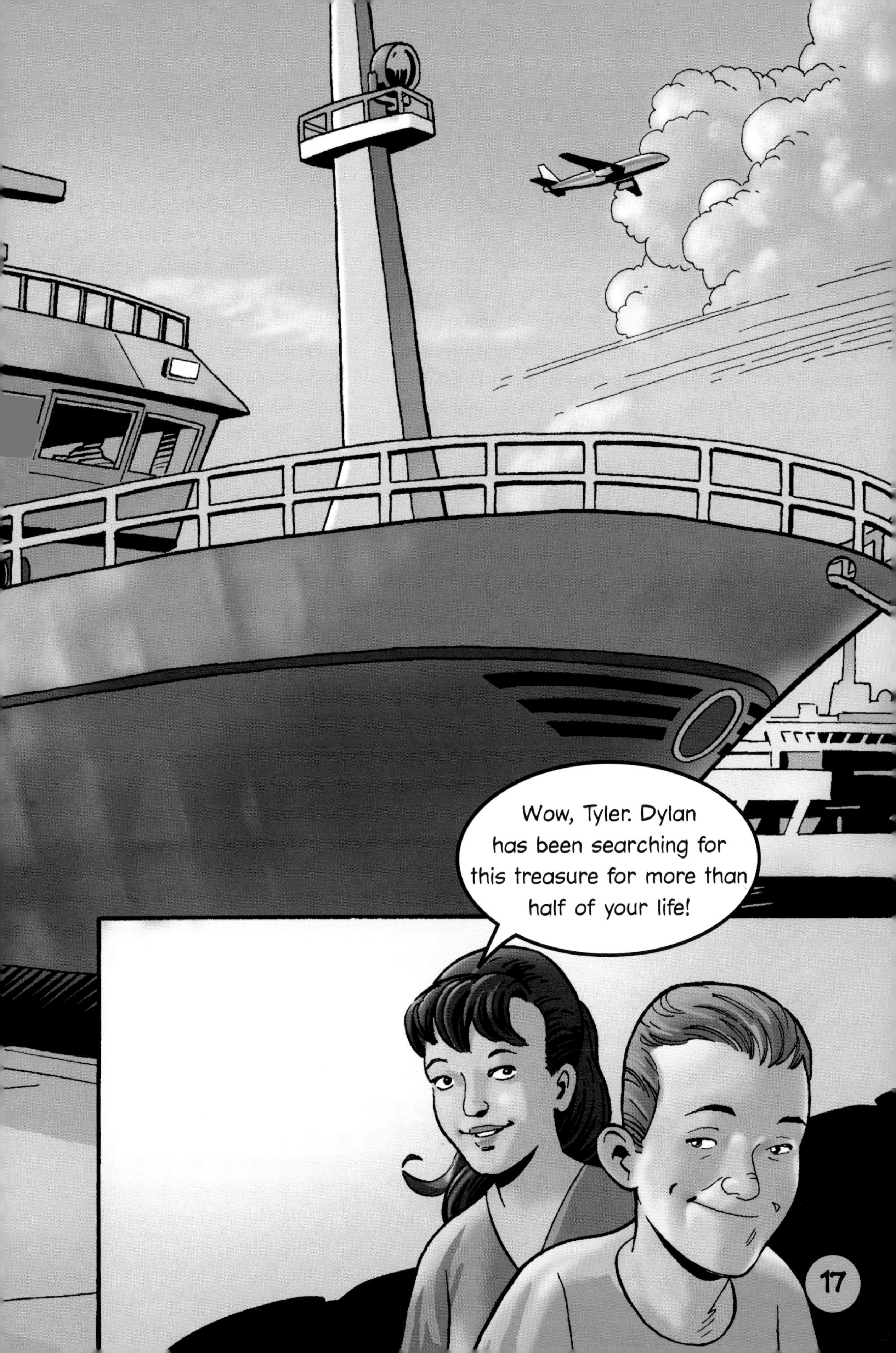
Wow, Tyler. Dylan has been searching for this treasure for more than half of your life!

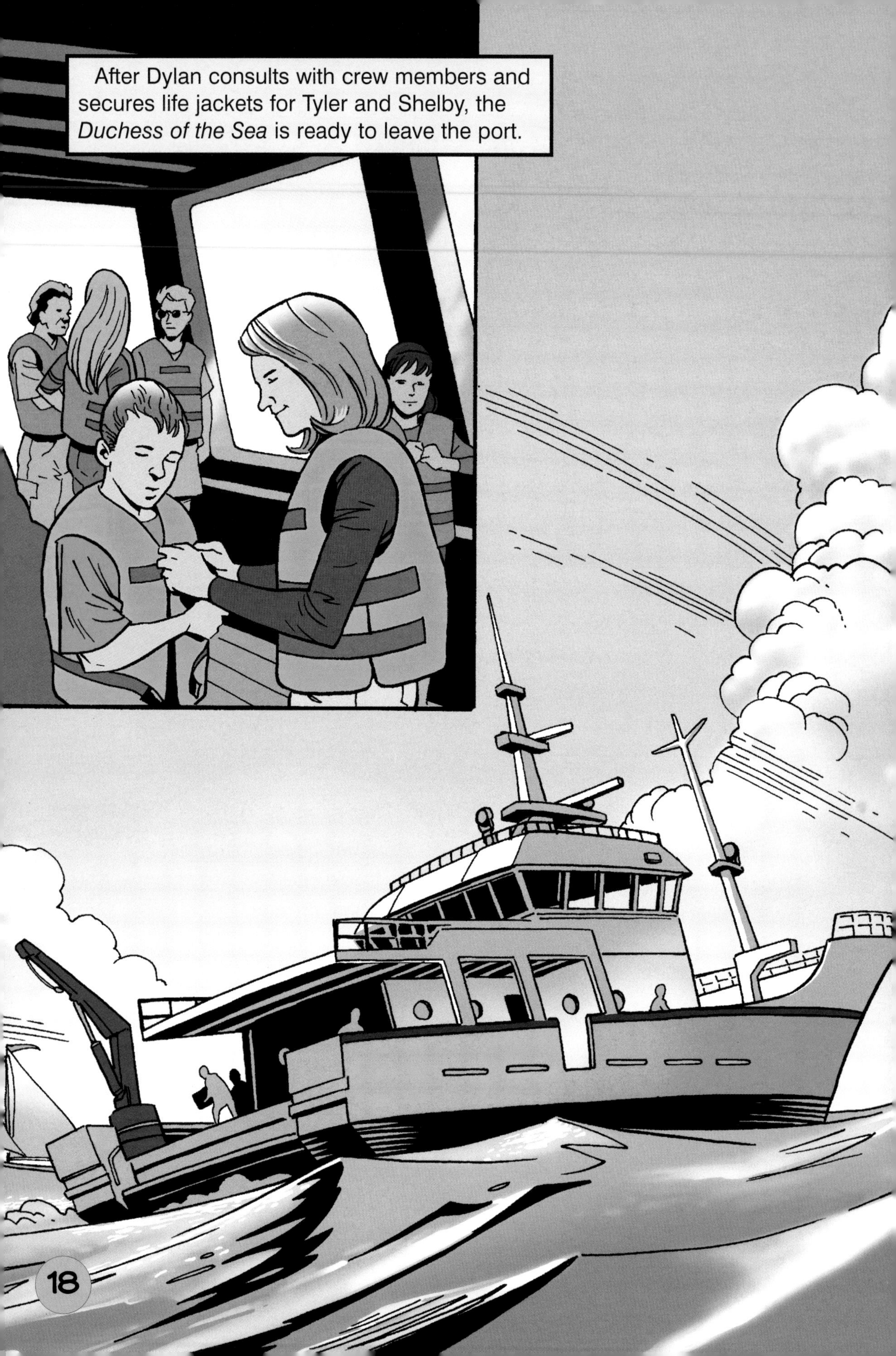
After Dylan consults with crew members and secures life jackets for Tyler and Shelby, the *Duchess of the Sea* is ready to leave the port.

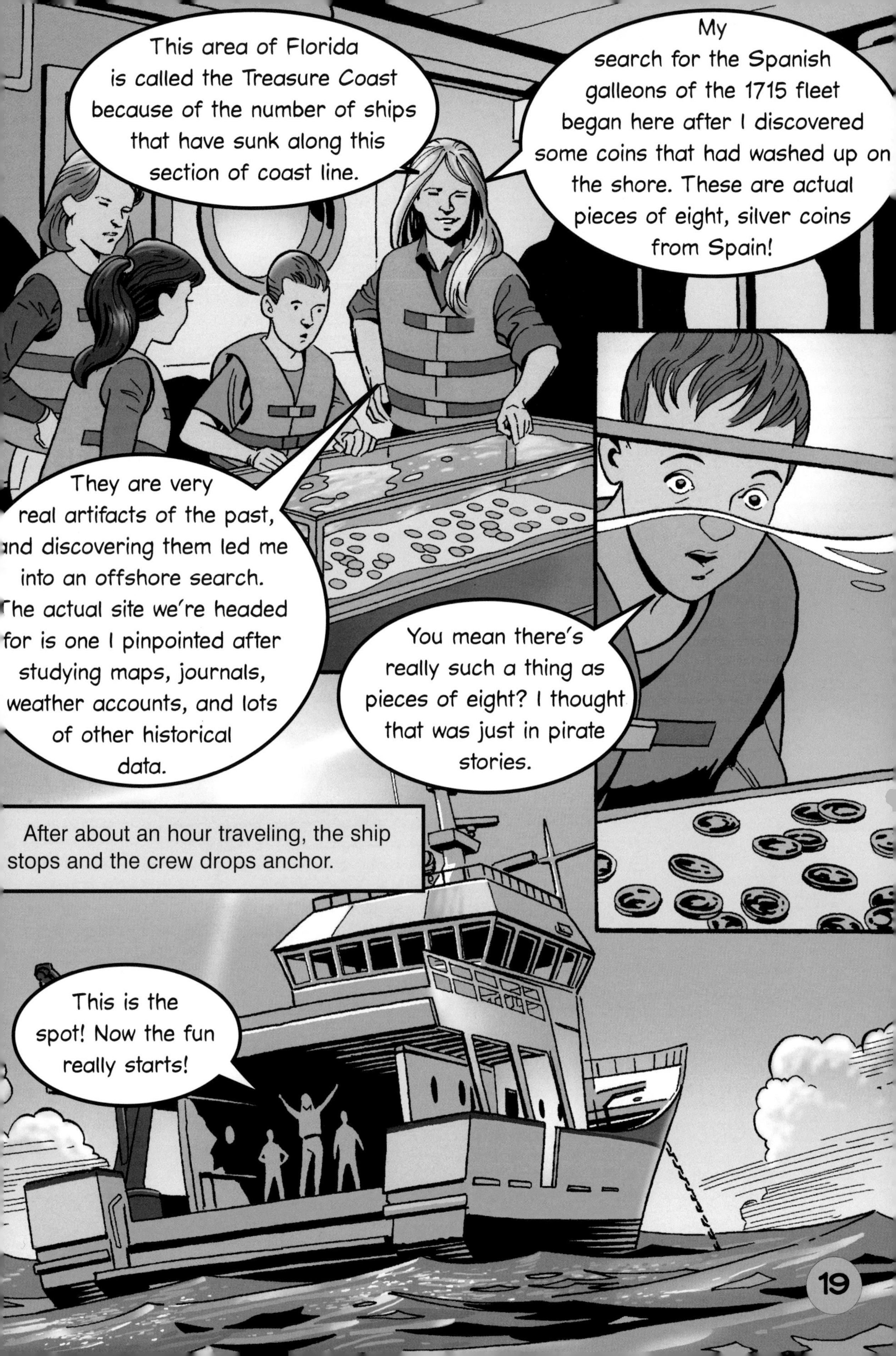
This area of Florida is called the Treasure Coast because of the number of ships that have sunk along this section of coast line.
My search for the Spanish galleons of the 1715 fleet began here after I discovered some coins that had washed up on the shore. These are actual pieces of eight, silver coins from Spain!
They are very real artifacts of the past, and discovering them led me into an offshore search. The actual site we're headed for is one I pinpointed after studying maps, journals, weather accounts, and lots of other historical data.
You mean there's really such a thing as pieces of eight? I thought that was just in pirate stories.
After about an hour traveling, the ship stops and the crew drops anchor.
This is the spot! Now the fun really starts!

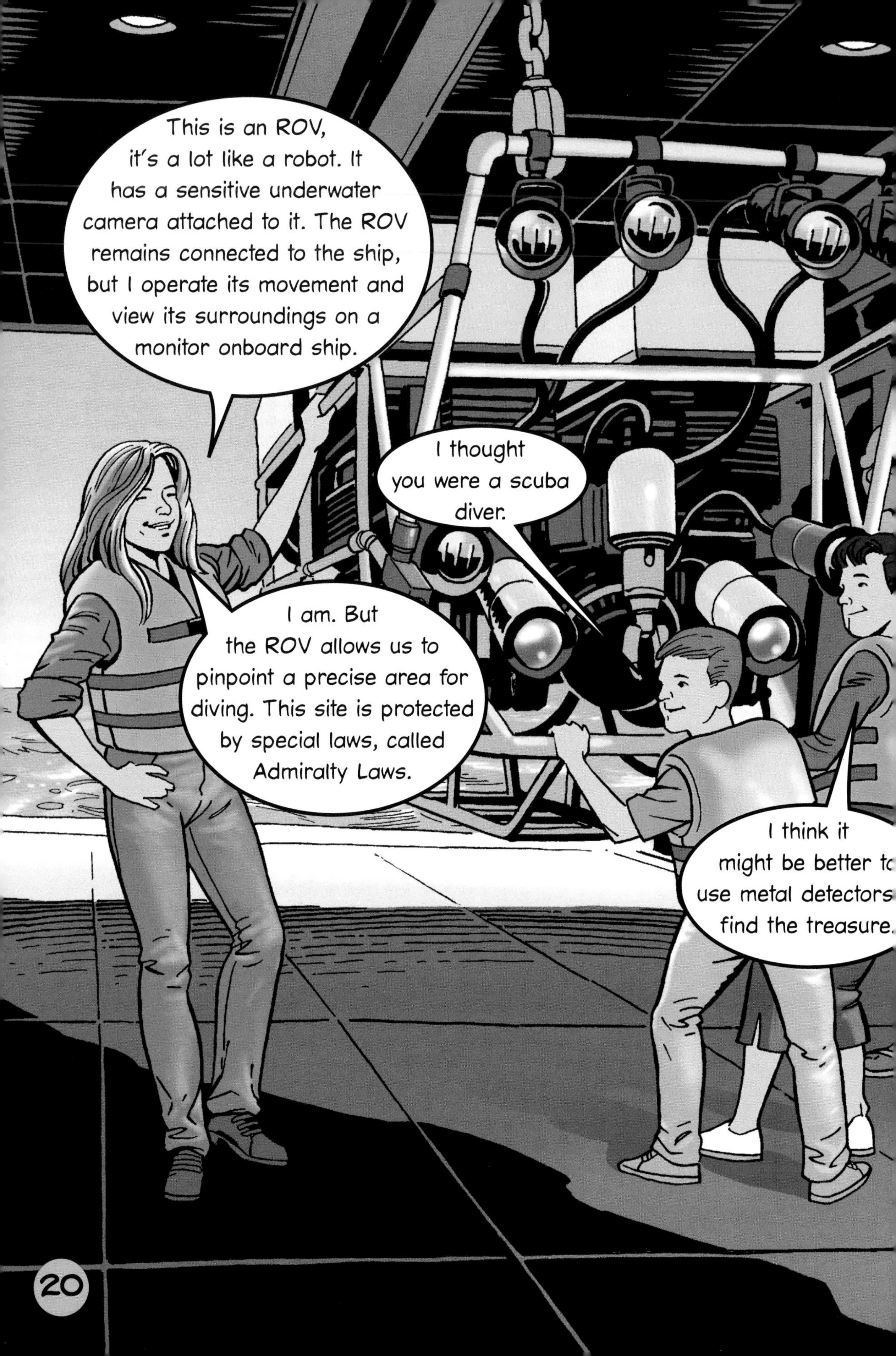
This is an ROV, it's a lot like a robot. It has a sensitive underwater camera attached to it. The ROV remains connected to the ship, but I operate its movement and view its surroundings on a monitor onboard ship.
I thought you were a scuba diver.
I am. But the ROV allows us to pinpoint a precise area for diving. This site is protected by special laws, called Admiralty Laws.
I think it might be better to use metal detectors find the treasure.

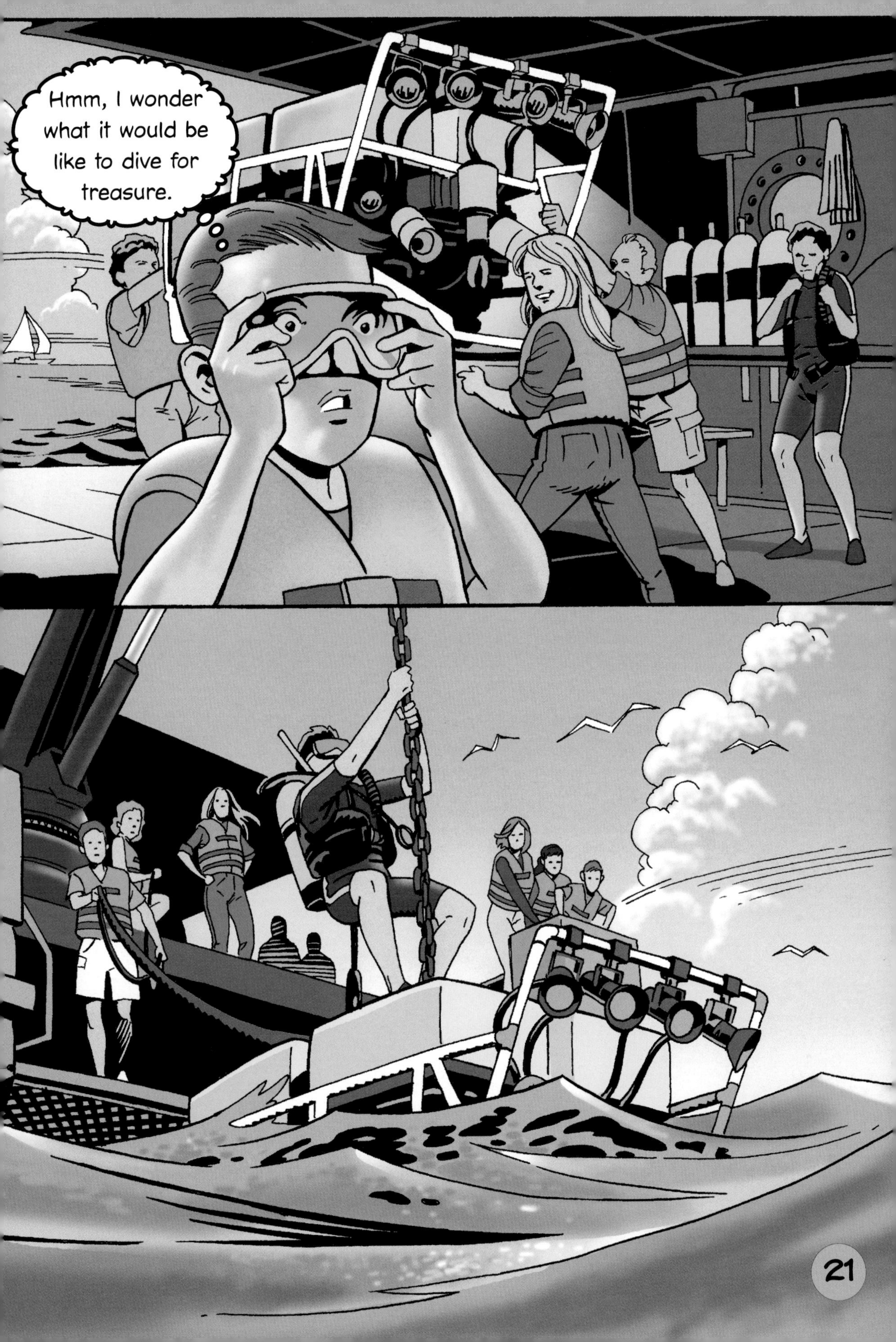
Hmm, I wonder what it would be like to dive for treasure.

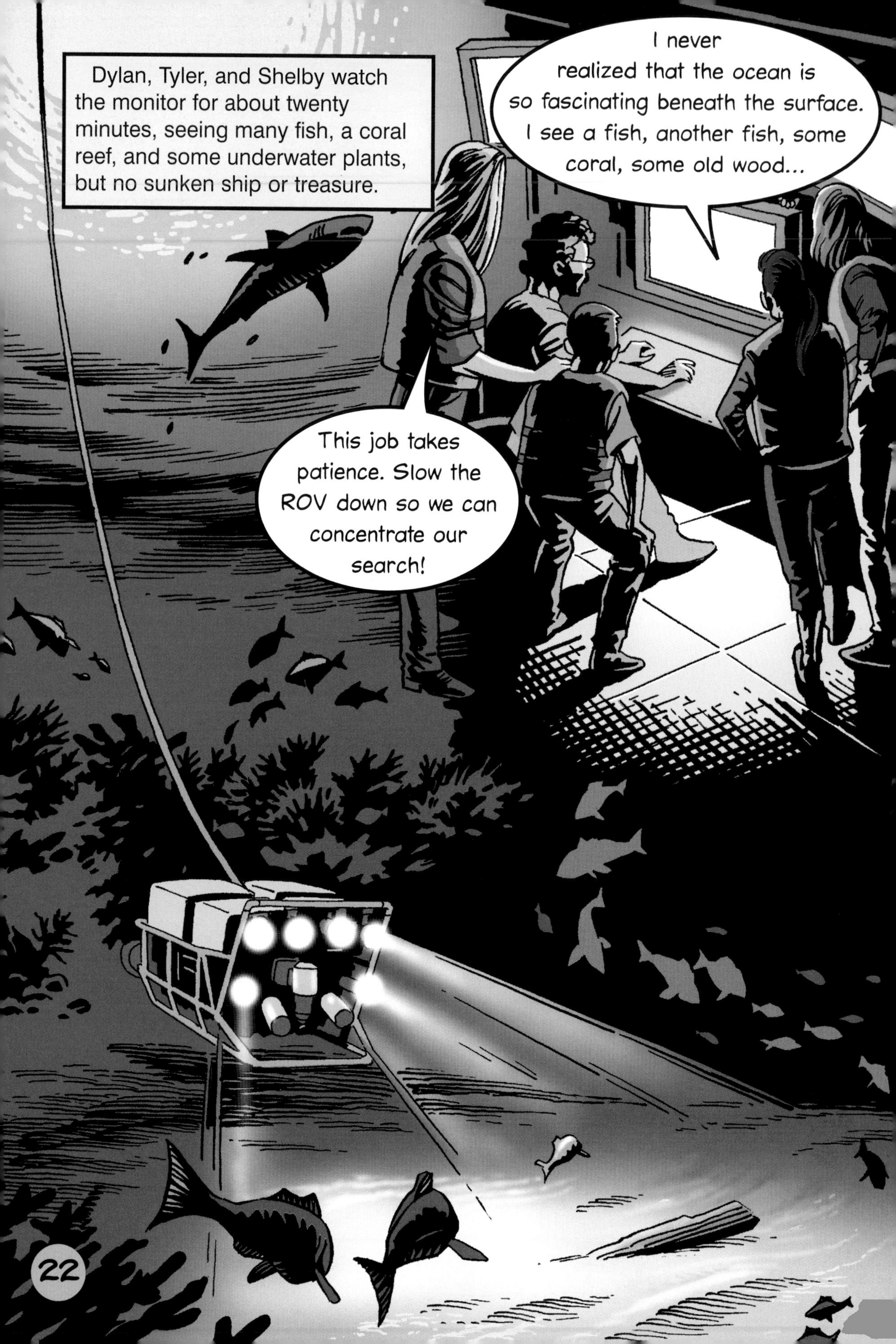
Dylan, Tyler, and Shelby watch the monitor for about twenty minutes, seeing many fish, a coral reef, and some underwater plants, but no sunken ship or treasure.
I never realized that the ocean is so fascinating beneath the surface. I see a fish, another fish, some coral, some old wood...
This job takes patience. Slow the ROV down so we can concentrate our search!

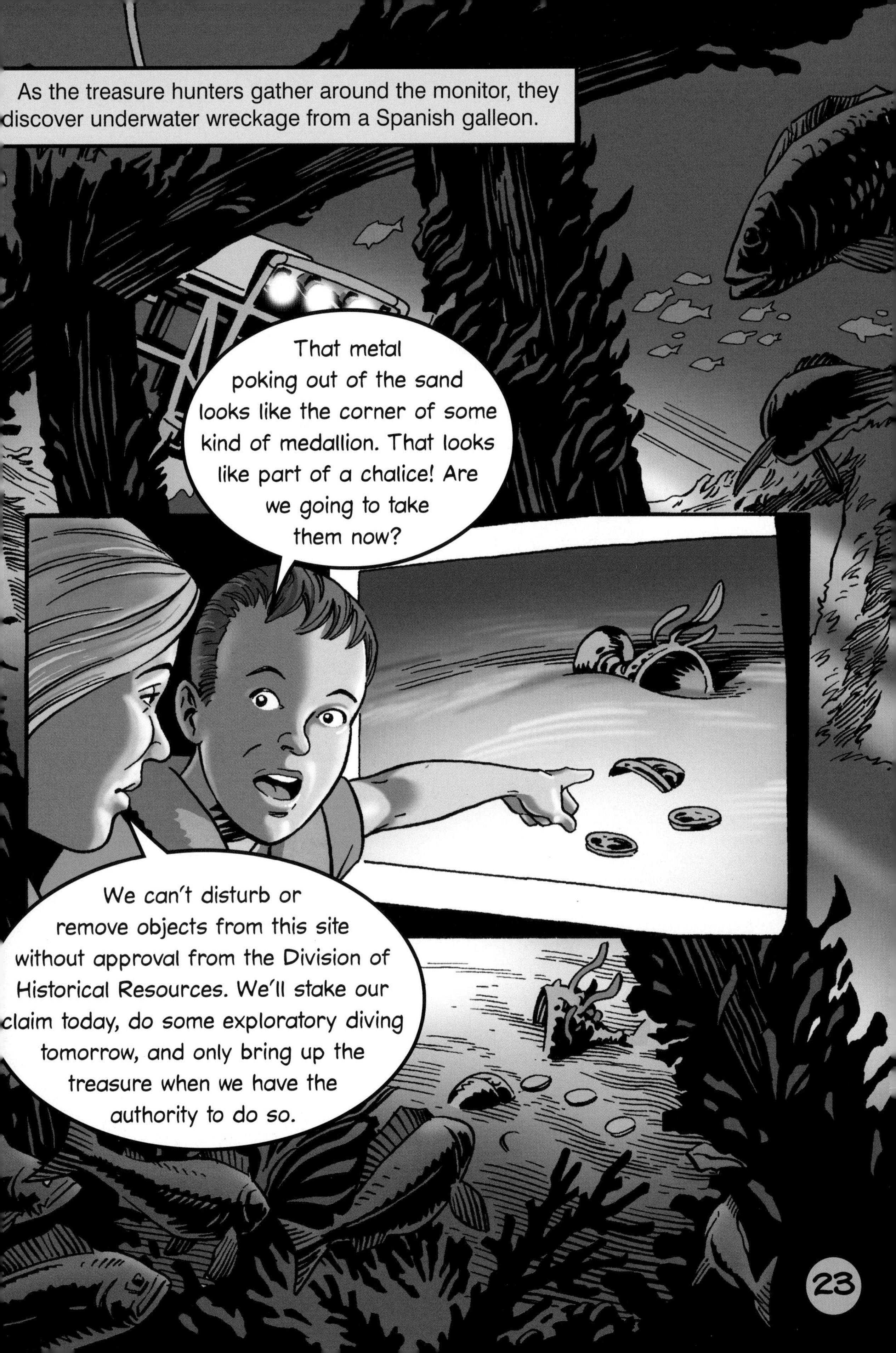
As the treasure hunters gather around the monitor, they discover underwater wreckage from a Spanish galleon.
That metal poking out of the sand looks like the corner of some kind of medallion. That looks like part of a chalice! Are we going to take them now?
We can't disturb or remove objects from this site without approval from the Division of Historical Resources. We'll stake our claim today, do some exploratory diving tomorrow, and only bring up the treasure when we have the authority to do so.

Several weeks later, Tyler and Shelby return to the *Duchess of the Sea* for the salvage mission. Mrs. West waits with them on the ship while Dylan and several other divers enter the water.

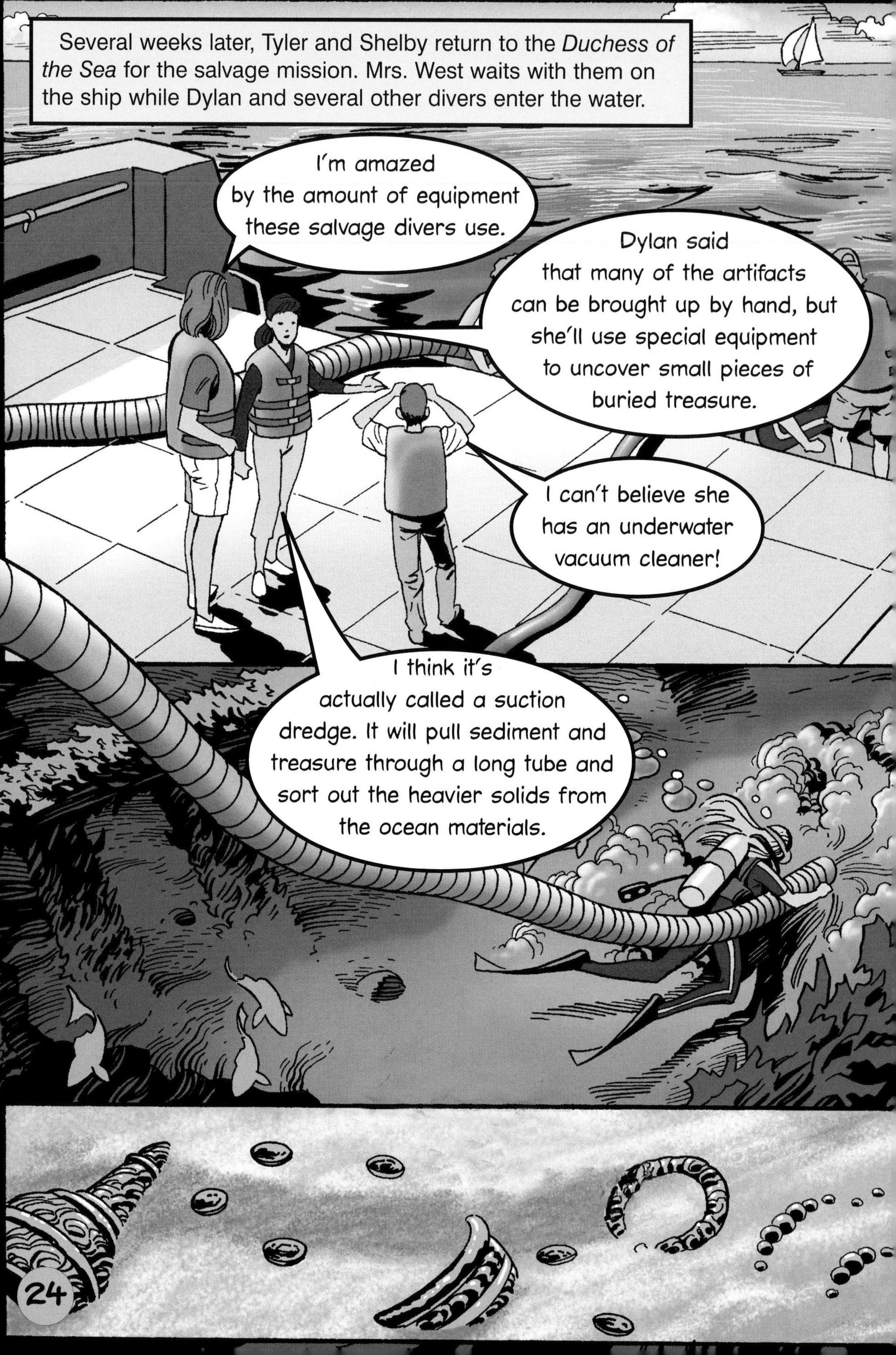
I'm amazed by the amount of equipment these salvage divers use.
Dylan said that many of the artifacts can be brought up by hand, but she'll use special equipment to uncover small pieces of buried treasure.
I can't believe she has an underwater vacuum cleaner!
I think it's actually called a suction dredge. It will pull sediment and treasure through a long tube and sort out the heavier solids from the ocean materials.

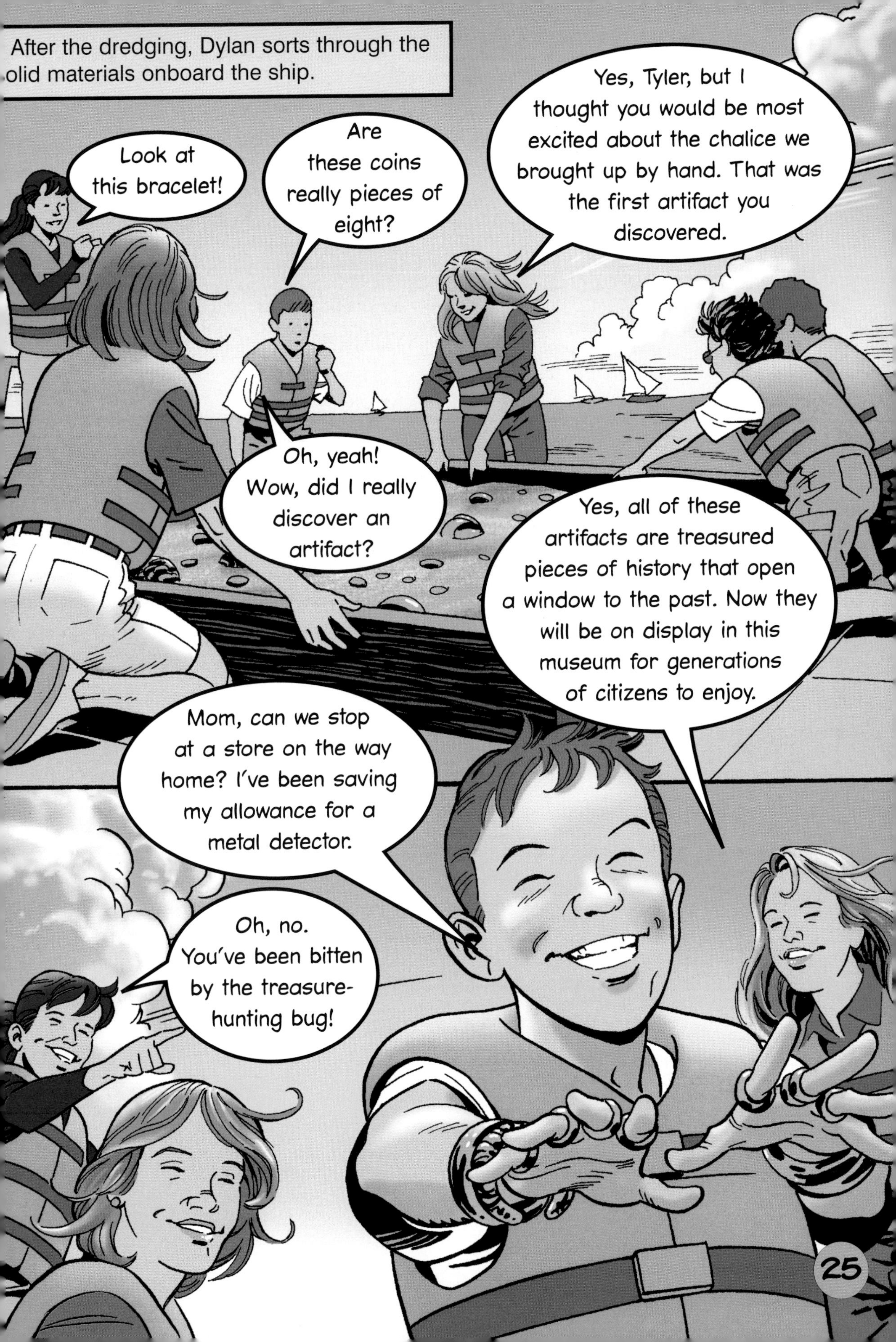
After the dredging, Dylan sorts through the olid materials onboard the ship.
Look at this bracelet!
Are these coins really pieces of eight?
Yes, Tyler, but I thought you would be most excited about the chalice we brought up by hand. That was the first artifact you discovered.
Oh, yeah! Wow, did I really discover an artifact?
Yes, all of these artifacts are treasured pieces of history that open a window to the past. Now they will be on display in this museum for generations of citizens to enjoy.
Mom, can we stop at a store on the way home? I've been saving my allowance for a metal detector.
Oh, no. You've been bitten by the treasure-hunting bug!

Shipwrecks

Shipwrecks hold more than gold, jewels, and rare coins. Shipwrecks can give us information about periods of history. They give us a peek into life on a Spanish galleon or on a coastal steamship. There are sunken British

Some of the most famous shipwreck discoveries have been valued in the billions of dollars!

warships, German U-boats, and Confederate blockade runners that can unlock mysteries of maritime war.

About 70 percent of the Earth's surface is covered with water. There are many areas yet unexplored, and many shipwrecks to be discovered. Off the coast of Florida alone, it is estimated there are possibly 5,000 shipwreck sites. Scuba divers and treasure hunters can stay busy around this peninsula for many years to come!

Salvage Diving

Salvage diving is an occupation devoted to recovering items from water. Sometimes a car runs off an icy road into a lake, or a fishing vessel is lost at sea. Salvage divers are trained scuba divers who find the sunken object and figure out the best way to bring it back to its owners. They often work with the Navy, the Coast Guard, or local law enforcement officers. Their jobs are important to police and members of the military. Sometimes salvage divers also discover ancient valuables in sunken ships. Salvage diving is a full time job that can be very rewarding.

Divers explore shipwrecks in oceans around the world as well as many of the Great Lakes in the United States.

Scuba

Scuba stands for Self-Contained Underwater Breathing Apparatus. It allows people to dive underwater and stay there for long periods of time by using the scuba equipment. Tanks filled with oxygen allow scuba divers to breathe under water while exploring an underwater scene.

Oxygen tanks might weigh 40 pounds (18 kilograms) or more, but feel weightless in the water.

Metal Detectors

People who like to search for treasure on land often use metal detectors. Metal detectors are electronic devices designed to locate metal objects that are buried underground. Some people use metal detectors to find lost objects in their own backyards, while others comb beaches in search of valuables hidden beneath the sand.

No one gets rich looking for treasure in the sand, but it can be fun!

ROVs

ROV stands for Remotely Operated underwater Vehicle, a device divers use to explore deep, underwater areas. ROVs usually have at least a video camera and lights attached to them. Cutting arms, water samplers, and measuring instruments might be attached as well to meet the needs of the scientists and ocean explorers using the ROVs. Cables connect the ROV to the ship and transmit information back and forth. ROVs can be small enough to hold in your hands, or as big as a small truck. ROVs are most useful in exploring unsafe diving sites and keeping other **submersibles** functioning properly.

Websites

all-kids.us/ship-parts-page.html

www.nps.gov/history/NR/travel/flshipwrecks/index.htm

dhr.dos.state.fl.us/archaeology/underwater/preserves

dsc.discovery.com/tv/treasure-quest/hsw/
    underwater-exploration.html

www.detecting.org.uk/html/Treasure_Hunting_
    Underwater_Metal_Detecting.html

Glossary

artifacts (ART-uh-fakts): Items created by humans usually for a practical purpose.

chalice (CHAL-us): This is a type of drinking cup or goblet.

fleet (FLEET): This is a group of ships operated under unified control.

galleon (GA-lee-un): In the fifteenth to early eighteenth centuries, this type of sailing ship was used by the Spanish for war or for commerce.

medallion (mu-DAL-yun): This is a large medal with an emblem or inscription engraved on it.

research (REE-surch): When someone is doing research, he is collecting information about a particular subject by reading about it or by performing experiments.

salvage (SAL-vij): This is the act of saving or rescuing a ship or its cargo.

submersibles (suhb-MUR-si-buhls): Machines that are able to explore deep, underwater areas that are too dangerous for divers.

swashbuckler (SWOSH-buk-lur): This is a swaggering or daring soldier or adventurer.

Index

About the Author

Susan Koehler is a teacher and a writer who lives in Tallahassee, Florida. As a child, she loved reading mysteries. She liked books so much that she gave up her recess time in elementary school to work in the school library. Beyond the pages of books, she enjoyed listening to stories about the colorful, real-life experiences of her parents and older siblings. Now she lives in a busy house filled with books, animals, and very funny children.

About the Artist

Shepherd Hendrix started his professional comics career in the early 1990s. His talents have led him into the world of animation and gaming as a conceptual designer and storyboard artist, collaborating with LucasArts and EA Games. Among his proudest works are with writer Derek McCulloch on the Eisner Award nominated *Stagger Lee* for Image Comics and *The Complete Idiot's Guide to U.S. History*.